How the Teachings of Jesus Could Save America

By Jason Newcomb

How the Teachings of Jesus Could Save America

By Jason Newcomb

LIGHT A CANDLE
BOOKS
Sarasota, FL

First published in 2008 by
Light a Candle Books
P. O. Box 18111
Sarasota, FL 34276
www.newcombcoaching.com

ISBN: 978-0-6152-0650-9

Cover Design and typesetting by LACB

15 14 13 12 11 10 09 08
8 7 6 5 4 3 2 1

Thank you to my wife Jennifer, for encouraging me to write down my thoughts in this way. I couldn't have done this without you.

Contents

INTRODUCTION
WHAT IS THIS BOOK?

When I look around at our nation in this moment of history, I see a society in terrible danger of disintegration. Problems plague our culture from every direction, rising hunger and poverty, a declining dollar, declining industry, growing personal debt, bankruptcy and foreclosure, constant violent crimes including senseless school shootings and other outrageous pointless acts, growing class and economic division, declining educational aptitude, disappearing codes of ethics and morality, all alongside massive legislative corruption, usurping of our freedoms and huge government debt.

On a more interpersonal level I see anger, resentment, greed, fear and mistrust operating in most of our interactions with our neighbors, and in our feelings toward government and even the media. Many people feel isolated and utterly alone in a cruel and violent world. In short, we are a culture deeply fractured, and we are walking together on perilously thin ice.

These are deep spiritual problems in our national, collective, and personal character. Many of us have lost touch with our spiritual core altogether. I have spent most of my adult life studying the functioning of human consciousness, along with the many and varied spiritual systems of the world. I have pondered the great existential questions, immersing myself in the great religious movements of both the

East and the West, as well as many of the more esoteric channels of spirituality throughout the world.

But as I look for solutions to the deep problems that face us as a nation, I come back again and again to the words of the young teacher from Nazareth. As I contemplate each of the problems that our culture faces I see the answers explained in such simple and elegant ways through the teachings of Jesus.

I have not written this book as a missionary for Christianity or an evangelist. Throughout my spiritual quest I have discovered many wonderful teachings about getting closer to God and living a meaningful life from all over the world. There are many useful teachings from many sources, both ancient and modern, that can help us live together in greater harmony and lead us toward peace, love and true brotherhood.

But the teachings of Jesus are some of simplest, most direct, and quite importantly, most familiar to Americans. In truth, many of the teachings of other cultures are very similar to those of Jesus. For instance, amongst the teachings of the Buddha we find phrases such as "Fools of little understanding are their own worst enemies, for they do wrong deeds which bear bitter fruits," or "As a solid rock is not shaken by the wind, so the wise are not shaken by blame and praise," or even, "But those who, when the truth has been taught to them, follow the truth, will pass over the dominion of death, however difficult to cross." These teachings and many others are quite similar in phrasing and intent to many of the teachings of Jesus.

In the Bhagavad Gita we find the following list of characteristics most of which will seem quite familiar to many Christians, "charity, sacrifice, study of the scriptures, austerity, honesty; nonviolence, truthfulness, absence of anger, renunciation, equanimity, abstaining from malicious talk, compassion for all creatures, freedom from greed, gentleness, modesty, absence of fickleness, splendor, forgiveness, fortitude, cleanliness, absence of malice, and absence of pride: these are some of the qualities of those endowed with divine virtues..."

Additionally, the first two limbs of Patanjali's yoga philosophy are quite similar in many respects to the Ten Commandments of Moses. In the practice of yoga one must not steal, or lie, or be envious and so forth. I could give hundreds of other examples, but few Americans have a copy of the *Dhammapada* on their bookshelves, or the *Bhagavad Gita,* or the *Tao Te Ching,* or the *Koran,* or the *Shiva Sutras* or any other lesser-known scripture that attempts to contain our collective wisdom.

But the teachings of Jesus are everywhere in this culture. His words are quoted and paraphrased throughout literature, film and television. His followers have buildings in every town, sometimes on nearly every corner of the town. A Bible can be found in most people's homes and even in most hotel rooms. The words of Jesus are everywhere. But this does not mean that his teachings are easy to follow, or that they are being followed by many of the people who today call themselves Christians.

The teachings of Jesus are quite challenging, and they have never been followed in any complete sense by any but a very few. Many Christians today find it very hard to follow the actual teachings of Jesus, and many churches do not even encourage their practice, instead focusing almost totally on faith in his death and resurrection as a path to salvation. But the teachings of Jesus actually indicate quite a different path. In Luke 6:46 Jesus says something quite clearly that seems almost like he could be speaking directly to many contemporary Christians.

> **And why call ye me, Lord, Lord, and do not the things which I say?**

In Matthew 7:21 he is even more explicit.

> **Not every one that saith unto me, Lord, Lord, shall enter into the kingdom of heaven; but he that doeth the will of my Father which is in heaven.**

By the "will of my Father" Jesus is most certainly indicating the teachings that he is currently giving, teachings which many Christians hold up as unattainable ideals rather than necessary practices. In Matthew 7:24 he emphasizes this even more clearly in the form of a parable.

> **Therefore whosoever heareth these sayings of mine, *and doeth them,* (emphasis mine) I will liken him unto a wise man, which built his house upon a rock:**

He then explains that when the rains come, the house of the wise man stands, whereas a person who hears his sayings and doesn't do them is like a fool that builds his house in the sand, so that it is washed away by the rain. Jesus clearly wanted all of his instructions to be followed, and these instructions provide a wonderful recipe for solving many of the troubles that we face as a nation.

This book will confine itself almost exclusively to the actual words of Jesus as they occur within the gospels. There are of course other stories and epistles that have been incorporated into the official canon of modern Christianity, many quite beautiful such as Paul's soliloquy on Love in First Corinthians. Many tenets of the modern faith are only found in these epistles, never mentioned by Jesus at all in his public ministry. But it is only the words of Jesus himself that we will focus on in this book, and not every word, but those that specifically relate to his teachings on ethics and morals.

Many contemporary secular scholars challenge the historical accuracy of the gospels or even the historical existence of Jesus at all. I will not undertake to explore these themes in this book. Rather we will explore the words of Jesus on their ethical, literary and spiritual merits alone. I used the King James Bible for all of the quotes in this book, because it is what I had at hand, and the most universally available. I have provided the verses along with all of the quotes in this book, and you may wish to look up the corresponding quotes from your favorite translation as you are reading. The message is pretty much the same in any translation, though perhaps a bit more clear in some of the most recent translations.

Whatever you think of the stories of Jesus, or of some of his followers past and present, the actual words that he spoke are filled with magic, mystery and wisdom. But not everybody cares for them. Some critics of the ministry of Jesus claim that his teachings are filled with naivete. These critics feel that his outlook on life and his expectations for humanity do not take into account the true depravity of human nature. While I agree wholeheartedly that we humans are capable of unthinkable acts of evil and destruction, I earnestly believe that we all do care about each other on some level, and that this goodness can be brought to the forefront if we choose to do so. I have seen many people engage in acts of kindness and pure generosity and I know that in our hearts we all long first and foremost to love and to be loved. The fact that our inherent goodness, and our basic loving nature, is often twisted throughout the course of life into cruelty, selfishness and corruption is not a refutation of the teaching of love and forgiveness. It is a call to arms that we must regain this goodness and learn to treat each other with the respect and love that we all desire and deserve.

We all have both good and evil within us, and it is up to each of us to choose the good. If we allow the fact that others are behaving badly to encourage us to do the same, we are dooming ourselves and the world. It is only by invoking the good inside each of us that we can hope to create a good and decent world. We must look to ourselves, and make sure that we are behaving justly, and from a pure heart. We must each take responsibility for ourselves, fearlessly acknowledging our own failings, and seeking to always make ourselves better. If we look at the world, and see its corruption, and allow that to excuse our own corruption then our lives become meaningless. It is not naïve to expect more of ourselves and to hope more for the world than we can presently see. It is visionary.

Critics of his teachings have also sometimes condemned Jesus as encouraging weakness. Nietzsche felt that Jesus taught the morality of the slave. This is largely because Jesus taught nonviolence, non-aggressiveness, and forgiveness of even the most horrible acts against us. Jesus himself did not even resist being crucified, but allowed himself to be murdered rather than giving up on what he believed in. But this is not weakness, quite the opposite, and I hope to show that quite clearly in the pages that follow.

The teachings of Jesus apply a different set of game rules than we traditionally use. When we look at people as basically in competition with one another, it seems that Jesus is asking us to allow people to walk all over us.

But Jesus is operating from a very different level, one in which there is no competition, because we are all ultimately one family, one indivisible unity, and that the suffering of anyone is the suffering of us all, the triumph of any of us is the triumph of us all. The universal love that Jesus taught takes us outside of any kind of conflict or competition. By these rules forgiveness of any error is only natural. By these rules it is inconceivable that we would wish to fight against one another or even to resist our own personal destruction. By these rules it would only be natural for any of us to say quite earnestly...

Father, forgive them; for they know not what they do.

Applying the teachings of Jesus as a mode of ethical and spiritual personal conduct requires incredible strength to undertake. But these teachings also deliver incredible power to those who do. It should be kept in mind that both Martin Luther King Jr. and Gandhi based their efforts to change the world on the model provided by Jesus. Both confronted injustice nonviolently, standing up to hatred and temporal power through the strength of their faith and the knowledge that their cause was more important even than their lives. Both ultimately met fates similar to Jesus, but their message likewise transformed the world forever. Those who apply the teachings of Jesus in their own lives usually have more impact on the world than almost anyone else. This is because the power of love positively inspires people much more than the fear created by force and aggression. When people act from a genuinely loving conviction the world takes notice and we are all ultimately enriched.

The words of Jesus are often quite simple, but the implications are almost always cosmic in scope. His message calls us almost automatically into a more mystic reality. Many of his propositions are really nearly impossible to accomplish if we are attempting to live up to them in everyday reality, such as his statement in Matthew 5:48.

Be ye therefore perfect, even as your Father which is in heaven is perfect.

Being as perfect as God does not really seem achievable while we are contending with the strife of the world around us. No matter how pure our intentions, we are often drawn back into conflict and upset. It is only when we enter into the loving mystical state of seeing beyond appearances, touching the timeless eternal, that we can get a taste of the perfection that Jesus prescribes.

Jesus also calls us to an absolute willingness to surrender all that we are and all that we have in Luke 14:33.

So likewise, whosoever he be of you that forsaketh not all that he hath, he cannot be my disciple.

Jesus wanted his disciples to be willing to sacrifice everything. This theme plays out more than once in the gospels. Although Jesus probably meant this quite literally, that his disciples should give up all possessions, positions, and ties to the world, becoming wandering seekers after the light, he certainly also meant it metaphorically and internally. We must forsake what we selfishly hold on to, our ambitions, our greed, our anger, our sorrow and everything else we cling to. Giving these things up takes us quite naturally into a state of mystical grace. Loving all things is automatic when we don't try to control or selfishly possess them. We see things as they are, rather than how we might like them to be, or how they could be better if we forced our will upon them. In the light of surrender, all things are perfect.

The idea of forsaking everything is quite disturbing when you are considering yourself at odds with the world around you. When you look at a violent and angry world it seems absurd to give up your small pleasures to seek after some distant truth, some kingdom of heaven in the sky. But Jesus imagined a different sort of life for his followers, and a different way of looking at the world.

Jesus wanted to free us from ourselves, from our burdens, fears, and pains. He wanted us to look at the world in a whole new light. In Matthew 11:28-30 Jesus gives us a glimpse of his vision.

> Come unto me, all ye that labour and are heavy laden, and I will give you rest. Take my yoke upon you, and learn of me; for I am meek and lowly in heart: and ye shall find rest unto your souls. For my yoke is easy, and my burden is light.

Jesus wanted to relieve us of our suffering by teaching us to see that we are all one human family, that the suffering of one of us is the suffering of is all. He wanted us to love each other unconditionally, and to forgive completely. Under these circumstances all needs disappear, and all conflict evaporates. Jesus was trying to teach us to be truly good people, to care about each other sincerely, and to live in harmony with one another and the world.

Some people today no longer believe in any kind of spirituality or metaphysical notions whatsoever and may ask why they should bother to be good at all, thinking that since there is no divine punishment for bad behavior, they may as well behave as poorly as they wish. But it does not matter whether you believe in a Supreme Being or not, being kind and generous is rewarding, and creates a better world. Being cruel and selfish makes a person bitter and cynical, and makes the world a little worse with each act of rottenness. But let's take a look at the teachings of Jesus themselves, and hopefully you will come to see what I am talking about.

CHAPTER 1
LOVE GOD, LOVE YOUR NEIGHBORS AND LOVE YOUR ENEMIES

Throughout this book I will refer to themes that will be familiar to many Christians, but I may offer a slightly different perspective or interpretation than the one that is familiar to you. I hope that you will be patient, understanding that I am trying to write a book that will present the message of Jesus to everyone. On the other hand, some of you reading this book may come from a non-Christian spiritual background, or from an agnostic point of view. I hope that you will be patient with the more spiritual elements in this book. I am not trying to convince you to accept any particular religious ideas. The message of universal love that Jesus shared with the world was not merely a religious idea, and does not require any particular spiritual belief system to be useful. Loving each other is still of the greatest relevance today, and key to our continued survival as a society.

The title of this chapter is central to the whole teaching of Jesus. If we are going to create a just and free society we must be kind to each other. Loving God and loving each other is the greatest gift we can give to ourselves and everyone around us. Many Christians today place far more importance on the death and resurrection of Jesus than they do on the message of love that he offered to us all and I think that is a great shame.

According to the gospels one of the learned theologians and lawyers of his time once confronted Jesus. This lawyer was interested in discrediting him. He asked Jesus which commandment was most important. The answer that Jesus gave in Matthew 22:37-39 was simple and beautiful.

Thou shalt love the Lord thy God with all thy heart, and with all thy soul, and with all thy mind. This is the first and great commandment. And the second is like unto it, Thou shalt love thy neighbour as thyself.

What more concise and eloquent message of universal love could there be? The most important thing that you can do is to love God with all of your heart, soul and mind. It is the essence of real existence itself. God is the supreme consciousness of the universe. God is the source of existence itself. And the next most important thing is to love your neighbor as yourself. Oh, if only we could all live this way, how much simpler and more pleasant life could be. In Mark 12:31 Jesus emphasizes the importance of these two concepts.

There is none other commandment greater than these.

And in Matthew 22:40, he states that these principles are the essential core of all the scriptures.

On these two commandments hang all the law and the prophets.

The idea of loving God is relatively easy for people who still retain some semblance of religious feeling in these trying times. If you believe in God, it is rather natural to feel a sense of gratitude to God for your existence. You are alive. The world is full of infinite possibilities. It is easy to love God when life is good. But many of us are caught up in personal tragedies and challenges that make us question the inherent goodness of God and the universe. This happens quite frequently these days. The challenges of the world are getting more and more constant, and the injustices that surround us are becoming more and more extreme.

However, it is at these very times when the belief in God and faith that things will ultimately get better can be most beneficial. But in order to really believe anything like this it is necessary to step out of the world of circumstances, and into the world of spirit. And the power to do so is within the instruction itself. If you focus your attention on God, loving God, dwelling in your love of God, your consciousness naturally takes on a more universal and cosmic nature. When you focus your attention on the eternal nature of God, the small circumstances of your little life take on their proper significance. Jesus repeatedly instructs his disciples to do just this, and we will talk about this further in upcoming chapters.

It is sad that so much of society has lost the basic ability to even believe in God, let alone to dwell in a state of love for God. I am fairly certain that it is a disbelief in anything beyond ourselves that has led to much of the pain and individual suffering in the world today. We have become an incredibly selfish and self-involved society. Selfishness has always existed, but now it is praised and rewarded openly. All sorts of villainy and corruption are admired in this country. Mass murderers frequently receive proposals of marriage while they are on death row. Corporate raiders and other cold-hearted profiteers are praised as heroes. The bottom line is more important than the lives of people who lose their jobs, homes, and families. This is a direct result of the selfishness and atheism that has spread over the last couple of centuries, and particularly in the twentieth century. Without a belief in anything beyond ourselves, most people have become interested only in themselves. This has caused greed, possessiveness, jealousy, anger and lust to now openly become the dominant drives within our culture. Most people in this world are entirely driven by the quest for success, money and social position. If spirituality plays a role in life at all, it is a very secondary role. And most people are willing to sacrifice just about anything for worldly success, even their own spiritual beliefs. But Jesus wanted something very different for us. In Mark 8:37 he asks some important questions.

> **For what shall it profit a man, if he shall gain the whole world, and lose his own soul? Or what shall a man give in exchange for his soul?**

Jesus did not want his followers to concern themselves at all with worldly position, money, power or any other earthly concern, instead focusing with all their hearts on finding and entering the kingdom of heaven.

However, as I said in the introduction, I am not trying to convert you to Christianity in this book, or even to religion at all. If you cannot believe in God for scientific or personal reasons, I am not going to try to persuade you otherwise. But if we are to create a just society, we must raise our personal standards, we must establish a code of personal morals and ethics, and abide by that code with all of our hearts.

Even if that code does not involve a belief in God, it must contain principles that are greater than our individual selves. When the entire focus of your life consists in trying to pay your rent or your mortgage, trying to attract sex partners, or striving to become a pop star, you find yourself at odds with the universe. You are a tiny player in a very big game. And it is a game that is largely stacked against you.

Even if you win this game, you still feel empty and alone. Why do you think so many celebrities end up dying of drug overdoses? It is simply because fame, fortune, adoration and all the other prizes of success do not make people happy. They have nothing to do with happiness. Don't get me wrong, some successful people are quite happy, but it is not merely because they have become successful. These people are already happy. Happiness and success have no causal relationship whatsoever.

The easiest way to create happiness for yourself, and more importantly a feeling of real satisfaction, is to have something that you are working on that is greater than yourself. Working toward a just cause, upholding and living a principle, trying to transform the world for the better, these paths lead to satisfaction. Because even if you fail to achieve them you know that you are doing something that is right and noble. And if you work toward such ends, the world will transform around you.

Let me give you an example. I know a young woman who was once very caught up in herself. She didn't believe in anything, and felt lonely and isolated. I tried to tell her about this idea that I'm trying to express to you now. I told her that if something is worth doing, we must commit ourselves to it wholeheartedly, even be willing to sacrifice our lives if necessary. It is better to die standing up for something that we believe in than to live believing in nothing.

She scowled and scoffed at me, telling me that dying for something that we believe would be stupid. She was sure that it was more important for her to live and try to get some little pleasure out of this life on earth than to sacrifice herself to some silly ideal.

Then she started to take a look around at the world we live in, noticing how the wealthiest people in society pull the strings of government and are slowly but surely taking away our freedoms. She noticed that most Americans are in debt and even servitude to the banks and the government tax collectors. She realized that if we don't do something about this soon we won't have any more rights or any more money at all. She thought about her daughter, and all the children that are growing up in this world, and realized that if we don't do something, the world they inherit will be a completely bleak and hopeless slave existence. She realized that much of her own helplessness, hopelessness and self-involvement were manufactured by these same bankers and government bodies. And she decided to do something about it. Not only that, but she decided that it would be worth sacrificing her own life if it meant that freedom and hope could be restored in the world. She discovered something bigger than herself, and her life suddenly took on real meaning.

Now she is working actively to free our society, and to educate others about the corruption all around us. This is her "kingdom of heaven," and she is focused on it with all her heart. Each of us must find the meaningful purpose that our lives will serve, to discover that thing which we would be willing to die for. Once you discover this, your power is infinite. It is greater than death itself. Jesus knew all of this, and alluded to it in his parable in Matthew 13:45-46.

> The kingdom of heaven is like unto a merchant man, seeking goodly pearls: Who, when he had found one pearl of great price, went and sold all that he had, and bought it.

Once you have found the meaningful purpose of your life, you will be willing to sell all that you have in order to obtain it. Nothing will be more important to you than that purpose. And that purpose will certainly be something you would willingly die for. Jesus emphasized this idea in Luke 17:33.

> Whosoever shall seek to save his life shall lose it; and whosoever shall lose his life shall preserve it.

Jesus wanted us to understand that when we act selfishly, when our goals are only selfish, when we just want to save ourselves, our lives are really pretty meaningless. When our goals are bigger than we are, when we are living by a higher principle, we have something that is more valuable than life itself.

But your goals may still not seem extraordinary, even if they are meaningful. Not everybody is destined to change the world in any outer way. Just living a principled, honest and loving life will change the world more than you can most likely imagine. As long as you are trying to be a good person, and trying to be helpful and loving to all people, you will become a force of positive transformation in the universe.

On the other hand some people may say that they know the purpose of their life, and that it is to become a rock star, or a professional athlete, or the most successful executive in the world. I assure you that if there is not some greater purpose behind such success it will deliver no more pleasure than doing nothing. There will be a temporary feeling of happiness, but emptiness will soon return. On the other hand, if you use your great success to champion a greater cause, or to live by higher principles, you will find that you are full of life, love and true meaning even if you fail or lose your career or even your life.

Even if you do not or cannot believe in God, realize that this concept of God can really be seen as the sum of all of our noble ideals, just causes, and worthwhile undertakings. God is the sum of all of these and the greater whole that is created by their union. God is all that is good in humanity, all that is beautiful in the universe, all that is sacred in our hearts. It is not necessary to adopt any particular belief system in order to want the world to be a better place, and if you devote yourself to that cause, you are doing God's work. Not only that, but each day will have meaning for you, each moment will be a treasure of great price that you cannot lose.

That is not to say that life is any easier when you devote yourself to a higher purpose. Sometimes it is extremely hard, and sometimes you will want to give up entirely. Even Jesus suffered doubt and despair at times, as in Luke 22:42.

Father, if thou be willing, remove this cup from me: nevertheless not my will, but thine, be done.

In Mark 15:34 while on the cross, Jesus cries out in utter anguish.

My God, my God, why hast thou forsaken me?

But Jesus did not give up on his principles, not even in the face of his own destruction. And in so doing, he transformed the world. You can transform the world too. Each of us must do our part to make the world a better place, by devoting ourselves wholeheartedly to a greater meaning.

The second teaching of Jesus is equally important.

Thou shalt love thy neighbour as thyself.

What does it mean to love your neighbor as yourself? There are two possible interpretations of this phrase. Either we are to love our neighbors as much as we love ourselves, or we are to literally love our neighbors as if they are ourselves. The end result is the same. We must give the same consideration to our neighbors that we would give to ourselves. Jesus even says this directly in Matthew 7:12.

Therefore all things whatsoever ye would that men should do to you, do ye even so to them...

Both of these last two quotes from Jesus can actually be found elsewhere in history. They occur in similar form in the Old Testament, as well as amongst the writings of the Greek philosophers. They are the core principles of a just society and the basis for the concept of human rights. The "golden rule" offers everyone equal dignity, respect and fair treatment. In order to have a truly good society we need to extend this respect to all people, whether or not we agree with their way of life, their choices or their views. We must allow others to live life as they see fit, and others must allow us to live our lives as we choose.

Some people have criticized this concept as simplistic or unattainable. The most common argument against "the golden rule" is that since different people have different expectations, it is surely impossible in practice for everyone to accommodate each other. For instance, some people might not mind being yelled at or even getting punched in the nose, and so feel free to yell at others or beat them savagely.

But we must not allow our own goodness to be damaged by someone else's lack of character. That is the fast path to ruin. If we behave badly because our neighbor is behaving badly then we have abandoned the "golden rule" completely. This is the opposite of what Jesus was trying to teach us.

If we each work toward our own ideal we will find unity within diversity. We are all one collective humanity, and we must love our neighbors as ourselves if we are to achieve a just society.

But what does this mean in practice? It means that we must be kind to one another. We must try not to engage in behaviors that cause unnecessary grief to each other. We must open our hearts in pure love to all that exists, transforming injustice through the power of moral strength, rather than through violence or oppression. This means allowing other people the freedom to do what they want to do, and not imposing our personal expectations on them. We can impose expectations on ourselves, but not on anyone else. Would you want your neighbor to tell you what you could and could not do?

This lack of basic respect for each other is a problem that runs very deep. Our society is currently imposing itself on its neighbors in a most uncharitable way. We are enforcing our will in the world through the weapons of war, economic control and political manipulation. Would we want other countries to be doing these things to us? Imagine if the Chinese army landed on our shore, overthrew our government, forbade other countries to trade with us, and installed a puppet dictatorship over our people. Would we want that? Would we put up with it? And yet we are doing just that all over the world.

It is a great mistake to say that we are right to invade other countries just because those countries are mistreating their citizens. It is not right to do evil in order to end evil. We must find a better and more just way to bring peace, happiness and universal prosperity to every corner of the world. There is injustice and suffering in many countries that we do not engage with militarily or politically. Many countries in South America, Asia and Africa have brutal dictatorships. China and Saudi Arabia have serious human rights problems. But our government does not interfere.

Our current choices are neither just nor inspired by a desire for justice. They are inspired by greed and power. We must love our neighbors as we would have them love us. Otherwise we will have perpetual war forever. The same holds true on an individual to individual basis. And we must extend this principle to the whole world, being good stewards of our natural environment and over all the many forms of life across our planet.

And Jesus took this concept much further, his expectations for a good neighbor went considerably beyond merely being nice to one another and not seeking to force our ideas on others. In Luke 10:30-37 he tells an important parable.

A certain man went down from Jerusalem to Jericho, and fell among thieves, which stripped him of his raiment, and wounded him, and departed, leaving him half dead. And by chance there came down a certain priest that way: and when he saw him, he passed by on the other side. And likewise a Levite, when he was at the place, came and looked on him, and passed by on the other side. But a certain Samaritan, as he journeyed, came where he was: and when he saw him, he had compassion on him, And went to him, and bound up his wounds, pouring in oil and wine, and set him on his own beast, and brought him to an inn, and took care of him. And on the morrow when he departed, he took out two pence, and gave them to the host, and said unto him, Take care of him; and whatsoever thou spendest more, when I come again, I will repay thee. Which now of these three, thinkest thou, was neighbour unto him that fell among the thieves? And he said, He that showed mercy on him. Then said Jesus unto him, Go, and do thou likewise.

If we want this world to be a better place, we must be truly good to one another. This means reaching beyond our comfortable living rooms and really trying to help each other. Many people feel that the world is degenerating, morals are disappearing; the poor are living in squalor and the rich in decadence. But if we merely stand in judgement over these problems in our society what will we accomplish? We must all reach out to our neighbors, offering food, clothing, support, friendship and love. Not to make an attempt at converting them to whatever religion we happen to support, but purely because it is the right thing to do from a pure heart. If you go out and truly love your neighbors you will be amazed at how quickly the world will transform. When we all begin to behave like one human family, when we realize that all of the world's problems are our problems, things will change.

It is unfortunate that so many people think that by merely convincing other people to change their religious views they will save the world. If we all say that we uphold a moral principle such as the "golden rule," but we uphold it only with our mouths while our hearts are inwardly condemning, judging and hating, how will the world be any better? If we live by the principles of love and forgiveness in our lives at all times, then the world will truly change.

Jesus realized that the world that surrounds us is imperfect, and that many in the world are not ready for his message of pure love for all that exists. That is why when he sent out his disciples he warned them in Matthew 10:16.

Behold, I send you forth as sheep in the midst of wolves: be ye therefore wise as serpents, and harmless as doves.

Jesus knew that universal love is not always greeted with open arms. Some people are so damaged that they become hostile when they are greeted with love, or try to manipulate goodhearted people into becoming servants. But Jesus knew that the answer to this problem is to love all people anyway, and to rise above even the most violent assaults, continuing to love without fail. Being "wise as a serpent" means understanding that even if our love is greeted with hatred, we must still continue to love, even if we must temporarily retreat, because love is the only way to conquer hate.

Jesus did not want us merely to be kind to our friends and acquaintances. He wanted us to be good to all people. He didn't want us to be charitable with only our fellow church members who are on hard times, but to be giving and loving to all. In Matthew 5:43-45 Jesus outlines a proposition that is rather hard to live up to, but is nonetheless essential if we are to create a good world.

> Ye have heard that it hath been said, Thou shalt love thy neighbour, and hate thine enemy. But I say unto you, Love your enemies, bless them that curse you, do good to them that hate you, and pray for them which despitefully use you, and persecute you; That ye may be the children of your Father which is in heaven: for he maketh his sun to rise on the evil and on the good, and sendeth rain on the just and on the unjust.

Jesus knew that just being good to people that we are comfortable with would accomplish little, but that doing good to everyone would accomplish real miracles. Many people think that they are living up to this principle by merely praying that this or that person will be "saved" as they have become saved, by accepting Jesus as their savior. But this is not what Jesus was talking about at all. Merely praying for a person to "get saved" is just judging them. You are deciding that someone else's life is somehow wrong or inferior and desiring to impose your belief system upon them. Would you want someone to impose their belief system upon you? Islam and Buddhism are growing in this world and may one day outnumber the adherents of Christianity, how would it feel to know that there are people who feel sorry for you and are praying for you to convert to their religion? How does it feel to know that atheistic materialists think you are stupid because of your primitive and hypocritical beliefs? This kind of judgement is not the behavior of a good neighbor.

No, if we are to truly adopt the teachings of Jesus it is necessary to do good to our enemies not in the hopes of swaying them over to our point of view or in an attempt to convert them at all. We must do it simply because we are good and noble beings who do good in the universe. Then we may consider ourselves the children of God.

Jesus shares this quite simply in Luke 6:32-34, explaining that we do not receive a just reward from the universe by doing things that are easy, but by doing things that are hard.

> For if ye love them which love you, what thank have ye? For sinners also love those that love them. And if ye do good to them which do good to you, what thank have ye? For sinners also do even the same. And if ye lend to them of whom ye hope to receive, what thank have ye? for sinners also lend to sinners, to receive as much again.

What Jesus is saying here is that if we only love those that love us, do good for people who do good for us, and give help to those who we expect help from at some future time we are not really doing good at all. We are just trading in a closed system, and nothing will change. The same people will love us, and the same people will hate us. But if we love those who hate us, and give of our hearts freely to people who behave badly the world will begin to change. Love is contagious.

But this won't always happen. Sometimes you will receive nothing, and the world will remain the same. Expecting the world to visibly change is entirely missing the point. So what is the real reward for doing good to all people, whether friends or enemies, without any expectation of changing them or getting anything at all in return? The reward is that you will be living by the most sacred principle in the universe. You will truly be doing good, and will discover the kingdom of heaven.

Jesus explains this in a parable in Matthew 25:34-40.

Then shall the King say unto them on his right hand, Come, ye blessed of my Father, inherit the kingdom prepared for you from the foundation of the world: For I was an hungered, and ye gave me meat: I was thirsty, and ye gave me drink: I was a stranger, and ye took me in: Naked, and ye clothed me: I was sick, and ye visited me: I was in prison, and ye came unto me. Then shall the righteous answer him, saying, Lord, when saw we thee an hungered, and fed thee? Or thirsty, and gave thee drink? When saw we thee a stranger, and took thee in? or naked, and clothed thee? Or when saw we thee sick, or in prison, and came unto thee? And the King shall answer and say unto them, Verily I say unto you, Inasmuch as ye have done it unto one of the least of these my brethren, ye have done it unto me.

CHAPTER TWO
THE KINGDOM OF HEAVEN

So what is this kingdom of heaven or kingdom of God that Jesus so frequently discusses in his teachings? In some places he seems to be literally talking about some future event in which an actual kingdom will be established. This is the point of view that conventional Christianity most often adopts. But more often Jesus seems to be talking about something far different. In the teachings of Jesus it seems that the kingdom of heaven is something imminent, perhaps just out of reach, but available at any time to all that grasp for it. This kingdom seems almost to be an idea, or perhaps a state of consciousness. This concept is put forth most directly in Luke 17:20-21. The Pharisees confront Jesus and demand to know when his kingdom of God is going to come. His answer is quite interesting.

The kingdom of God cometh not with observation: Neither shall they say, Lo here! or, lo there! for, behold, the kingdom of God is within you.

The kingdom of God is within us? This shifts the meaning of the kingdom of God quite dramatically from the conventional definition. What kind of Kingdom exists inside us? Is it an imaginary Kingdom?

I don't think so. I don't even think he is speculating about mystical reveries or inner experiences.

I frequently meditate, so it is tempting to imagine that Jesus is telling us that we must meditate in order to find an inner kingdom of heaven. But I think Jesus is talking about something else when he says that the kingdom of God is within you. He is talking about the kingdom of God we co-create together when we lead a life of love, forgiveness, and pure-hearted charity toward everything. This is the kingdom of God that is within each one of us, and that we each bring into manifestation one tiny particle at a time with every act of genuine goodness.

Don't get me wrong, there is certainly a distinct, subjective, metaphysical experience that we can also call the kingdom of heaven. Many mystics, myself included, have experienced the light and beauty of the direct presence and union with the divine. This is surely the kingdom of heaven or God as well. Jesus mentions this place in John 18:36.

My kingdom is not of this world...

But it is the kingdom that we all help create through noble and gracious acts toward each other that Jesus refers to most frequently in his ethical teachings.

And ultimately these two kingdoms are one in essence. This is because we are not actually creating something new when we co-create the kingdom of heaven. We are revealing to others and ourselves something that is eternal and indestructible. We are manifesting the timeless, infinite core of goodness within us all. Since this book is about the teachings of Jesus, we will focus first and foremost on the kingdom as he taught it to his disciples and followers.

Most frequently, Jesus refers to the kingdom of heaven through parables. A number of these parables refer to growth, particularly plant growth, such as the parable found in Mark 4:26-29.

> So is the kingdom of God, as if a man should cast seed into the ground; And should sleep, and rise night and day, and the seed should spring and grow up, he knoweth not how. For the earth bringeth forth fruit of herself; first the blade, then the ear, after that the full corn in the ear.

The seed Jesus called "the word of God." By this he meant the good and noble, loving behavior that he was prescribing through his teachings. By planting the seed of goodness in the world through our acts of love and kindness, the kingdom of heaven begins to grow around us. He expresses this again in Matthew 13:31-32.

> The kingdom of heaven is like to a grain of mustard seed, which a man took, and sowed in his field: Which indeed is the least of all seeds: but when it is grown, it is the greatest among herbs, and becometh a tree, so that the birds of the air come and lodge in the branches thereof.

Even though the seed (or good deed that you do) may be small, the tree (or divine kingdom) that results will be bigger and more beautiful than you can imagine. This is clearly not a literal kingdom that Jesus is describing at all, but rather a divine ideal or state of being that we draw toward ourselves through aspiring to be perfect. Jesus also uses a baking metaphor to express this same kind of idea in Matthew 13:33.

The kingdom of heaven is like unto leaven, which a woman took, and hid in three measures of meal, till the whole was leavened.

These parables remind me of a movie from a number of years ago, called "Pay it Forward," in which a young boy suggests that we do good deeds for one another, and for every good deed that we receive, we give one to someone else. This seems to be the essence of what Jesus is communicating here. By being good people, we spread goodness in the world. And even if we receive no reward directly, or our goodness has no direct effect, we are still transforming the universe through our goodness. Even if our good efforts result in us being attacked or hated, we are still spreading good in the universe, even if it doesn't seem so immediately. Jesus expresses this in Matthew 5:10.

Blessed are they which are persecuted for righteousness' sake: for theirs is the kingdom of heaven.

Those who behave righteously with no hope of reward co-create the kingdom of heaven with each noble act, even if their goodness is punished rather than rewarded. We must not be good just in the hope of creating a perfect world because then we are just trying to bargain with the universe, trying to sell our acts of goodness to try to get something even better. In doing this we will inevitably fall, because the world will not always seem to become any better when we do good. Sometimes it may seem to get worse. Sometimes we may end up getting killed by the forces of tyranny and superstition. These negative forces exist within us all, and are often triggered in reaction to those who seek to change the world through love.

Instead, we must simply be good to each other without any hope that it will benefit us at all. We must be good for the sake of being good. It is only by doing this that the world will really change, whether we get to enjoy the change or not. This is somewhat paradoxical, but it is nonetheless true, because our goodness *is* the change.

In the above, Jesus is also referring to the metaphysical heaven that you can experience in mystical visions of fullness. This mystic kingdom is opened in precisely the same way. By opening our hearts, we are drawn up into the mystical reality of the divine. He states this quite simply in Matthew 5:8.

Blessed are the pure in heart: for they shall see God.

They shall see God both through a mystical experience of the perfect divine reality that exists beyond our normal awareness, but also directly in the world by seeing that everything partakes of the goodness of the divine. When your heart is pure everything is beautiful. Jesus also refers to both a metaphysical and imminent kingdom of heaven in two parables that describe great treasures, one of which I quoted in the last chapter, the parable of the pearl of great price. In Matthew 13:44 he tells a similar parable, which further indicates the great value of our good and noble behavior, and how we must be willing to and desire to give up everything else in order to obtain it.

Again, the kingdom of heaven is like unto treasure hid in a field; the which when a man hath found, he hideth, and for joy thereof goeth and selleth all that he hath, and buyeth that field.

Jesus further describes the kingdom of heaven with a fishing metaphor in Matthew 13:47-48.

> Again, the kingdom of heaven is like unto a net, that was cast into the sea, and gathered of every kind: Which, when it was full, they drew to shore, and sat down, and gathered the good into vessels, but cast the bad away.

This parable is particularly interesting because it describes something of the nature of the force of good. It is like a net, a matrix of goodness that draws everything together. Everything that is unworthy falls away.

Some may say that my interpretations about the kingdom of heaven are sweet-natured but ill-conceived, because in other places Jesus also vividly describes the end of the world in calamity before the coming of the kingdom of heaven. These descriptions of hellfire and worldwide destruction occupy the imaginations of many Christians when they consider the kingdom of heaven. In places the descriptions of Jesus certainly seem to foretell bad things coming, the apocalypse, and punishment for the damned. Jesus also discusses the idea that the kingdom of heaven may come when we least expect it, so it is important to be in a state of readiness.

The end of the world may be coming in a literal sense, or it may not. The kingdom of heaven may be established after a worldwide destruction, or perhaps it is already here. It is not my wish to challenge anyone's theological convictions, but rather to offer an additional possible interpretation that can be viewed side by side with any other beliefs.

THE KINGDOM OF HEAVEN

There are also other ways of interpreting the apocalyptic descriptions of Jesus and the account in John's revelation which are more mystical than historical. This matter is beyond the scope of this book.

Keep one thing in mind, Jesus describes destructive world events in a fair degree of detail, but in describing these events, Jesus also says this in Mark 9:1.

> Verily I say unto you, That there be some of them that stand here, which shall not taste of death, till they have seen the kingdom of God come with power.

Jesus said that some of the people that were listening to him at that time would see the kingdom of God before they died. But whoever was standing there listening to Jesus say these words has certainly been dead for nearly two thousand years. And the world has never come to an end in a fiery conflagration of angels and brimstone. There are really only two ways of interpreting this. Either Jesus was wrong, or he was talking about something slightly different than the literal end of the world. In fact, in Luke 9:27 the passage is worded somewhat differently.

> But I tell you of a truth, there be some standing here, which shall not taste of death, till they see the kingdom of God.

In this passage Jesus seems to be referring to something that is available at any time, something that we can see as soon as we are ready. The kingdom of God is always with us, for those who have eyes to see and ears to hear.

CHAPTER THREE
FORGIVENESS AND JUDGEMENT

This world does indeed seem to be degenerating. Murder, rape, incest, theft, corruption, oppression and a thousand other crimes against each other plague our cities and towns. One of the most important things that we can do as a society is to raise our moral standards. But we cannot hope to raise the moral standards of anyone but ourselves. And this we really need to do. We must each strive to be the most loving and giving people that we can be if we want to create a better world.

Instead of standing in judgement over anyone else's choices we can only raise our own standards for ourselves and spread goodness by the example of our own goodness. Telling others that they must behave according to our expectations of goodness is not goodness at all. It is oppression. This is not an act of loving your neighbor and takes us further and further from the kingdom of heaven. And it also violates another central teaching of Jesus from Matthew 7:1-2.

Judge not, that ye be not judged. For with what judgment ye judge, ye shall be judged: and with what measure ye mete, it shall be measured to you again.

Even if you do not believe in a Supreme Being to act as judge, please know that this statement is still true. Giving up judgement is a reward in and of itself. This is because by standing in judgement over others you are creating the conditions for you to be judged by others. And when you are judged by others you will be forced by your own interior psychological patterning to accept this judgement, at least on some level, because you too have judged.

If you do not judge others, then if others judge you it will be meaningless because judgement will be meaningless to you. When you are able to look upon your fellow beings without judgement you see them as brothers and sisters, as essential parts of yourself, and their judgement is easily forgivable. In one of his most famous quotes, Jesus illustrates the obvious fallacy of judging our brothers and sisters in John 8:7.

He that is without sin among you, let him first cast a stone at her.

If someday you are really "without sin" you will still not judge, but instead you will forgive just as Jesus did. You may not agree with every choice that others make for them- selves, but you must allow others to make their choices. If their choices seem to be evil or unjust, be an oasis or a sanctuary for your brothers and sisters rather than a court- room.

Let everyone you meet know that you love them, and that you will listen to them without judgement. Then you will become trusted, and eventually your own goodness will become transformational. But if you tell people that their way of life or their behavior is evil, you will only cause them to be more distant, more lost.

Besides, who are you to judge whether something is right or wrong? Leave such judgement aside. Instead behave as Jesus prescribes in Luke 6:36.

Be ye therefore merciful, as your Father also is merciful.

Jesus also teaches this same lesson in Matthew 5:7.

Blessed are the merciful: for they shall obtain mercy.

Jesus also pointed all this out in a well-known teaching from Matthew 7:3-5 that has all but been ignored in practice in most people's lives. But this teaching is of the utmost importance if we are going to create a free and loving society.

And why beholdest thou the mote that is in thy brother's eye, but considerest not the beam that is in thine own eye? Or how wilt thou say to thy brother, Let me pull out the mote out of thine eye; and, behold, a beam is in thine own eye? Thou hypocrite, first cast out the beam out of thine own eye; and then shalt thou see clearly to cast out the mote out of thy brother's eye.

By 'mote" Jesus means a small speck or sliver of wood. It is a metaphor for the small transgressions that we perceive in others. By "beam," Jesus means a huge log of wood, a metaphor for the huge inconsistencies and transgressions in ourselves. Instead of focusing on the problems of others, Jesus wants us to instead focus on how we can improve ourselves. Then, once we are perfect and only then, can we consider offering help to others. And this help will not consist of judgement, but instead love, under-standing and most importantly forgiveness.

Peter once asked Jesus how many times he should forgive his brother if his brother sinned against him. Jesus answered him in Matthew 18:22.

I say not unto thee, Until seven times: but, Until seventy times seven.

In other words, Jesus expects us to forgive people completely without question or complaint over and over again. In Mark 11:25-26 Jesus explains this in a similar manner to judgement.

And when ye stand praying, forgive, if ye have ought against any: that your Father also which is in heaven may forgive you your trespasses. But if ye do not forgive, neither will your Father which is in heaven forgive your trespasses.

Just like judgement, forgiveness does not require a belief in anything supernatural in order to be effective. It is its own reward. When you forgive others, whether you think they have harmed you or have just offended you in some way, you release the tension created by the event, and can move more freely toward a state of love. Forgiveness frees both the person who is forgiven and the person who forgives equally. Both can then move more easily toward love.

In order for this to work you must really forgive the person and really let the matter go. And if you forgive something really big, your reward will be really big, both in terms of releasing your own tension and in the amount of gratitude you will produce in the person you forgive. Jesus states this quite nicely in a parable from Luke 7:41-42.

> There was a certain creditor which had two debtors: the one owed five hundred pence, and the other fifty. And when they had nothing to pay, he frankly forgave them both. Tell me therefore, which of them will love him most?

CHAPTER FOUR
THE MAMMON OF UNRIGHTEOUSNESS

Many modern Christian preachers like to say that God wants us to be successful and rich, and that we should focus on obtaining riches in our prayers. But in reality Jesus had many unfavorable things to say about money, the rich, and those who spend their time seeking to be rich. He refers to money as "Mammon" in several of his teachings, which is most often considered the personification of money and riches as a demon. Jesus held the poor in very high esteem, with statements such as these in Luke 6:20-21

Blessed be ye poor: for yours is the kingdom of God. Blessed are ye that hunger now: for ye shall be filled.

On the other hand, Jesus held a very low regard for the rich.

But woe unto you that are rich! for ye have received your consolation.

Jesus taught that people who focus their time on building wealth are not building a real relationship with the highest. Rich people receive only the empty and often temporary consolation that money brings, and not the spiritual rewards of a life dedicated to true principle. He tells his followers quite explicitly in many places to stay away from the pursuit of money, as in Matthew 6:19-20.

> Lay not up for yourselves treasures upon earth, where moth and rust doth corrupt, and where thieves break through and steal: But lay up for yourselves treasures in heaven, where neither moth nor rust doth corrupt, and where thieves do not break through nor steal: For where your treasure is, there will your heart be also.

This last sentence is quite illuminating. Where your treasure is, your heart is. If you spend all of your time focused on accumulating wealth, your heart will always be dwelling on protecting that wealth and accumulating more. There may be little or no real room for your connection with God or higher principles. How many rich people do you think would really give all their money away to devote themselves to living a pure and loving life? But this is exactly what Jesus prescribes in Mark 10:21.

> One thing thou lackest: go thy way, sell whatsoever thou hast, and give to the poor, and thou shalt have treasure in heaven: and come, take up the cross, and follow me.

Jesus suggests this same course in Luke 12:33-34, which also then connects with the theme in the previous quote from Matthew.

> Sell that ye have, and give alms; provide yourselves bags which wax not old, a treasure in the heavens that faileth not, where no thief approacheth, neither moth

corrupteth. For where your treasure is, there will your heart be also.

Jesus expected his followers not to focus on money at all. It is somewhat ironic to think about the televangelists today who focus so intensely on gathering money, or the preachers who tell their congregations that God wants them to be rich so they should "pray on money" to obtain success in life. Jesus wanted his followers to focus only on the highest principles, on loving all people with a pure heart, and that any and all needs would be provided for those who did so.

When we are focused on a higher purpose, the things that we need in order to obtain that purpose just become available as needed. On the other hand, when we are focused on our fears about how the bills will be paid or where our next meal is coming from all of our problems seem to be magnified. This can actually be even worse for the rich and spoiled who often feel like their world is crashing around them when the slightest inconvenience comes up, such as their reservations at the restaurant getting misplaced, a clerk in a store putting their items in the wrong bags, or their nail polish getting chipped. This sort of self-obsession takes us far from our ideals, far from loving-kindness, and ultimately leads to deep unhappiness. But the conveniences and empty pleasures provided by wealth and luxury make it very hard to disentangle yourself from this obsession. In Mark 10:24-25, Jesus directly addresses the problem with wealth.

Children, how hard is it for them that trust in riches to enter into the kingdom of God! It is easier for a camel to go through the eye of a needle, than for a rich man to enter into the kingdom of God.

This is not to say that it is absolutely impossible for a wealthy person to become devoted to the highest. It is just very, very unlikely because of the great stresses and temptations of money. Jesus' next statement expands on this idea further.

With men it is impossible, but not with God: for with God all things are possible.

Many theologians try to use this statement as an excuse for focusing on wealth. In their estimation, as long as we have faith in God, we can still spend all of our time obsessing about money, because with God all things are possible. So, it is even possible that through our belief alone we can be let into the kingdom of heaven even though all we do is obsess about money all week and then spend an hour on Sunday thinking nice thoughts about God.

But this is not what Jesus was saying at all. Jesus was simply saying that it might be possible for a rich person to lead the life of goodness and universal love that he was preaching if they really and truly focused entirely on God instead of their wealth. But it would be easier for a camel to pass through the eye of a needle than for anything like that to occur. In Matthew 6:24 Jesus explains why it is so hard for the wealthiest to enter into the kingdom.

No man can serve two masters: for either he will hate the one, and love the other; or else he will hold to the one, and despise the other. Ye cannot serve God and mammon.

Here we see Jesus identifying money with the demon Mammon. Jesus also warned us not to be jealous of others' earthly wealth. In Luke 12:15 he explains that life is simply not about wealth. To think that life is about wealth traps us in the true poverty of a life without meaning.

Take heed, and beware of covetousness: for a man's life consisteth not in the abundance of the things which he possesseth.

It was not money in and of itself that Jesus preached against. It was what money does to us that concerned Jesus. Money makes us idle and luxurious. Money makes us feel more important than those who have less. Or it can make us feel less important than those who have more. Money makes us think that we can manipulate and coerce our fellow human beings. All of these things carry us far from the ideal that Jesus wished for us.

And Jesus took this idea much further than merely wealth. Jesus wanted us to stop focusing on all earthly matters, letting these matters take care of themselves. Jesus wanted our lives to be completely dedicated, in love and bliss, to our higher purpose with no worry for anything else at all. Jesus expresses this quite clearly and simply in Matthew 6:34.

Take therefore no thought for the morrow: for the morrow shall take thought for the things of itself.

He also explains this idea in a series of poetic utterances that explain how and why we should not worry about the needs of life. Jesus saw the infinite abundance of the universe, and knew that we need not concern ourselves with anything but the highest. In Matthew 6:26 he explains why we should not worry about feeding ourselves.

> Behold the fowls of the air: for they sow not, neither do they reap, nor gather into barns; yet your heavenly Father feedeth them. Are ye not much better than they?

If the abundance of the universe can take care of the needs of birds, surely the universe will take care of all of us. In Matthew 6:28-30 he states that we do not even need to worry about clothing ourselves.

> And why take ye thought for raiment? Consider the lilies of the field, how they grow; they toil not, neither do they spin: And yet I say unto you, That even Solomon in all his glory was not arrayed like one of these. Wherefore, if God so clothe the grass of the field, which to day is, and to morrow is cast into the oven, shall he not much more clothe you, O ye of little faith?

The ideal that Jesus taught was far from our usual societal conventions. He wanted us first and foremost to focus on spreading his word of love, peace, tolerance and mercy.

By doing so we will all be brought into a state of unity. When we look upon others with the same love and care that we look upon ourselves, we are infinitely rich, even if we have nothing of earthly value. Our riches are in our hearts. They are in heaven, where they are eternal and indestructible. Nothing is more valuable than feeling good. And the easiest way to feel good is to be a loving person.

Jesus had nothing of earthly value in his life, and wanted his followers to follow his example. In Matthew 8:20 he explains the state of his own affairs.

The foxes have holes, and the birds of the air have nests; but the Son of man hath not where to lay his head.

In Luke 14:33 he explains his expectations of his followers.

So likewise, whosoever he be of you that forsaketh not all that he hath, he cannot be my disciple.

Jesus wanted us to give up our desire for earthly possessions entirely. He wanted us to forsake everything, and devote ourselves completely to the life of universal love that he prescribed. In Mark 8:34 he expresses the same basic idea, including the fact that we must even be willing to sacrifice our very lives in order to follow Jesus.

Whosoever will come after me, let him deny himself, and take up his cross, and follow me.

Our lives on this planet are but a blink of the cosmic eye. Soon our bodies will return to dust. Is it better to spend that moment on greed, selfishness and desire, or on loving all that you see? In Luke 12:16-21 Jesus tells the story of a rich man who spends all his time and energy thinking about his own wealth, and no time on the spirit.

The ground of a certain rich man brought forth plentifully: And he thought within himself, saying,

What shall I do, because I have no room where to bestow my fruits? And he said, This will I do: I will pull down my barns, and build greater; and there will I bestow all my fruits and my goods. And I will say to my soul, Soul, thou hast much goods laid up for many years; take thine ease, eat, drink, and be merry. But God said unto him, Thou fool, this night thy soul shall be required of thee: then whose shall those things be, which thou hast provided? So is he that layeth up treasure for himself, and is not rich toward God.

When we focus exclusively on material matters, we are robbing ourselves of the most important aspects of life, love, spirit, connection and higher principles. When our lives do eventually end, all that we have accumulated becomes meaningless, and all that we have ignored is what we find ourselves caring about. If we don't have love in our lives we realize that we have nothing. This is true poverty, poverty of the spirit. In Luke 12:31-32 Jesus explains that if we seek the highest, all that we need will be there for us, and infinitely more.

But rather seek ye the kingdom of God; and all these things shall be added unto you. Fear not, little flock; for it is your Father's good pleasure to give you the kingdom.

Jesus is not saying that focusing on the kingdom will deliver us earthly wealth. He is saying that spreading love and compassion in the world will provide us with spiritual wealth, a kingdom of heaven that is indestructible and eternal. And this is what God wants for us.

Jesus proposed an exciting challenge and adventure to humanity. He wanted us to stop striving against one another, and to start working together to be forces of goodness and love in the world. He knew that being concerned with money and possessions would stand in the way of this mission, because these things divide rather than unite us. Some people are more rich, others less rich. This cannot be avoided. Even in communist countries where wealth is supposed to be entirely shared, some people inevitably end up with much more than others. Jesus wanted his followers to stop concerning themselves with anything but spreading his message of universal love and compassion. In such a world everyone will be blessed with more than enough. When you focus on positive forces, you get positive returns. Imagine what the world would be like if everyone focused on spreading spiritual wealth to everybody, and stopped trying to hoard worldly wealth at all.

Now, I am not proposing that we all quit our jobs and become penniless wanderers. That would serve little purpose. But those amongst who are wealthy can begin to use those riches purely to build a better and more loving world. Those who have less can stop worrying so much about their position in society and instead focus on being good to each other and spreading love in the world.

Even if we do not give up our homes, automobiles, flat screen TVs, gold teeth, and meals at expensive restaurants, we must come to realize that these items do not provide the real meaning in our lives. It is in our relationships with each other, our own meaningful contributions to the universe, and offering love and goodwill to everyone that provides us with real wealth.

CHAPTER FIVE
HYPOCRISY AND THE LAW

All people have a tendency to obey cultural and divine laws in word only, while inwardly seeking ways to circumvent and get away with breaking these laws. Many people also make public displays of piety or nobleness simply to impress other people rather than out of an honest desire to be good people, but ultimately operate from a very unloving place. Jesus talks about this kind of hypocrisy more than almost any other topic.

These and other forms of hypocrisy are still with us today, and cause some of the greatest challenges to our collective welfare. Many people still spend the bulk of their energy trying to impress each other, either with their wealth and prestige, or with their outward show of goodness while being corrupt inside. In Luke 16:15 Jesus addresses this sort of person directly.

> Ye are they which justify yourselves before men; but God knoweth your hearts: for that which is highly esteemed among men is abomination in the sight of God.

These are rather harsh words, but the problem is obvious. If you are trying to show others how great you are, you are not focusing on your own goodness at all. You are not focusing on God. You are focusing on trying to win favor with other people. This is setting yourself against these other people, and ultimately leaves you feeling uncertain and alone. If you spend your time trying to prove how good you are, your heart will not be filled with genuine love at all. It will be filled with worry and doubt. Did I prove how noble I really am to him? Did I give enough to that charity to be considered a real philanthropist? These concerns separate you from your connection with the highest entirely. Jesus discusses this in Mark 7:6.

> **Well hath Esaias prophesied of you hypocrites, as it is written, This people honoureth me with their lips, but their heart is far from me.**

People tend to talk about their faith or their goodness much more than they actually live by these principles. This creates a terrible world in which everybody is pretending to believe in something, while not really doing it at all. It is obvious to most people that everyone else is being a hypocrite too, so many people judge each other for the very lack of character that they have in themselves.

Many politicians and spiritual leaders are caught doing improper things, many times the very things that they spend their sermons preaching about such as soliciting prostitutes, strange sex acts, gambling, or molesting children. Many modern spiritual leaders are the biggest hypocrites of us all.

Jesus knew that his proposition of actually living by the principles of love was somewhat dangerous because the vast majority of people live their lives in hypocrisy. Rather than honestly trying to be good and decent people, or even powerful people, most people spend their lives trying to make sure that others are aware of their good qualities.

Jesus knew that by proposing a genuine path to goodness he might appear to be challenging the current laws. So, in Matthew 5:17 he explains his position.

Think not that I am come to destroy the law, or the prophets: I am not come to destroy, but to fulfil.

He was not interested in getting rid of the current expectations, but rather to make sure that people were fulfilling them completely, and from a place of genuine integrity, love, and respect for all beings.

It is of the greatest importance that we behave in loving ways purely because we are loving beings, not because we have been told to do so. Hypocrites who appear to be upstanding citizens are not doing themselves or the world any good. In the end their hearts are filled with malice and greed, and they will never experience the real joy of pure love. If we behave well for the wrong reasons we may as well just behave badly. If our hearts are bad, it doesn't matter what we do. We are still bad on the inside, and it is what we are inside that defines our spirit.

At the time that Jesus was teaching, many sects of Judaism were outwardly following the laws of Moses, but inwardly they were corrupt, filled with greed and treachery. There are still many people like this today. How many people regularly attend church but behave badly for the rest of the week? How many people mistreat their spouses, pollute and litter, break laws, are ungenerous, unloving, unforgiving, judgmental, steal, and lie, but still call themselves Christians? Jesus spoke to these people directly in Matthew 5:20.

> For I say unto you, That except your righteousness shall exceed the righteousness of the scribes and Pharisees, ye shall in no case enter into the kingdom of heaven.

How can we create a good and decent world when we constantly behave so inconsistently? We must raise our standards within ourselves if we are to survive as a society. We must discover the seed of goodness that is within us all, and act from this goodness.

Jesus discussed several of the commandments of Moses in his teachings, and augmented them to show how even the least of transgressions against the better parts of our nature threaten to pull down the whole edifice of goodness within us. In Matthew 5:21-22 he discusses the commandment "thou shall not kill."

> Ye have heard that it was said by them of old time, Thou shalt not kill; and whosoever shall kill shall be in danger of the judgment: But I say unto you, That whosoever is angry with his brother without a cause shall be in danger of the judgment.

It is not enough to merely not kill with our hands or weapons. We need to rid ourselves of anger, hate, blame and judgement altogether. These are the silent killers. If we spend our time thinking ill of one another we are spreading death and hatred with every thought. Instead we must learn to accept each other without exception, forgiving each other's faults and working ceaselessly to be good to each other.

In Matthew 5:27-28 Jesus discusses the commandment "thou shalt not commit adultery."

Ye have heard that it was said by them of old time, Thou shalt not commit adultery: But I say unto you, That whosoever looketh on a woman to lust after her hath committed adultery with her already in his heart.

If we focus our energy on our lusts in this way, we are not being loving at all. That is not to say that we must become blind to beauty, but rather that we should not allow our minds to obsess about actions that are not in harmony with the choices we have made, and the people to whom we have committed our lives. It is only natural to appreciate attractive members of the opposite sex, but if we focus our energy on fantasizing about them incessantly we are robbed of our own highest purpose. The same holds true for other things beyond merely lusting after lovers. If we spend our days wishing that we had a different career, or a nicer car, or anything else we are not focusing on love, or a meaning- ful life. When we do this we are seeking to replace meaning with some other experience or possession. This takes us further and further from the divine. This brings us nothing but emptiness and more desire.

If we instead focus our energy on creating a better and nobler world, all of our desires will be fulfilled quite automatically. If we simplify our desires, so that our only real desire is to be good, then we will find it easy to accomplish our desires. All that we need to do in that case is simply to be good and all of our desires are instantly fulfilled.

Jesus discusses several other laws throughout his teachings, but the most challenging of his propositions comes in Matthew 5:38-40.

Ye have heard that it hath been said, An eye for an eye, and a tooth for a tooth: But I say unto you, That ye resist not evil: but whosoever shall smite thee on thy right cheek, turn to him the other also. And if any man will sue thee at the law, and take away thy coat, let him have thy cloak also.

This is one of the most famous doctrines of Jesus, and one of the most controversial. As I mentioned in the introduction, many interpret this instruction as encouraging weakness, that we are to allow ourselves to be abused and subjugated by others. Jesus then continues his thought in Matthew 5:41-42.

And whosoever shall compel thee to go a mile, go with him twain. Give to him that asketh thee, and from him that would borrow of thee turn not thou away.

Jesus is proposing that we consistently do more than is asked of us, and that our generosity should exceed all expectations. If someone wants something from us, we should give it, and even more. After all, we are all one family. This theme appears again in Luke 6:30, in an even more extreme manner.

Give to every man that asketh of thee; and of him that taketh away thy goods ask them not again.

Jesus wanted us to give everything to each other without question. He wanted our generosity and love for one another to be complete and all encompassing.

If we continue to view ourselves as existing in opposition to others, certainly these instructions tell us to be weak, to be slaves, to lack self-esteem or self-worth. But that is not the intention of Jesus at all.

These instructions can only be viewed in their proper light when we recognize that Jesus is instructing us to live a different kind of existence, an existence filled with love and a sense of unity with all things. When viewed in this way, these instructions are directions to have incredible strength.

Jesus is telling us that even if our brothers and sisters physically beat us, we must still view them as essentially ourselves, and continue to love them so much that we allow them to strike us again and again if they need to. He wants us, under all circumstances, to continue loving them and to continue on our path to the highest. If our clothing or our money or even our bodies are taken away from us, we can still love our brothers and sisters all the same.

We can do this because it is the love that is important, the giving and the compassion. These acts create a more beautiful world. Our bodies and our lives are secondary to the importance of our principles.

We can only enter into such a state when we are totally committed to the outcome of our highest ideals, when we are so dedicated to the path we are walking that we would gladly surrender anything, even our lives to see it accomplished. This is the greatest strength, and requires absolute integrity to accomplish. The world transforms around men and women who live this way.

If we must strive against some injustice in the world, we can do so nonviolently and non-judgmentally, by recognizing the essential unity that we share with our brothers and sisters. Then when we are resisting an evil, even if that evil uses one of our brothers or sisters to savagely beat our bodies or take away everything earthly that we possess, we can keep standing up and smiling. We can keep loving our brothers and sisters, and the strength of our love will conquer any evil eventually, though our bodies may be broken and maimed. War is practically inconceivable to anyone who wishes to live by the teachings of Jesus.

Jesus took this proposition very seriously, and made the rewards and repercussions quite clear in Matthew 5:19.

Whosoever therefore shall break one of these least commandments, and shall teach men so, he shall be called the least in the kingdom of heaven: but whosoever shall do and teach them, the same shall be called great in the kingdom of heaven.

He knew that living a life fearlessly dedicated to a higher purpose was indeed a challenging proposition. He knew that many would not be able to have the strength, or the capacity for love required to accomplish a life like this. But he also recognized that this was the only way to create a good and beautiful world.

And if a few can live this way, the world will begin to change. Each person who lives their life dedicated to love and the highest principles of equality, forgiveness and compassion has more impact on the world than one hundred thousand people who lead lives of selfishness and fear. He knew that only a few could accomplish the kind of love and strength that he proposed. He wanted his disciples to be among those few, but in Matthew 7:13-14 he seems aware that not all of them would be capable of this strength of character.

Enter ye in at the strait gate: for wide is the gate, and broad is the way, that leadeth to destruction, and many there be which go in thereat: strait is the gate, and narrow is the way, which leadeth unto life, and few there be that find it.

Jesus knew that it is all too easy to lead a life of selfishness and fear. The world encourages us to behave this way. This is the "wide gate." Living a life of love and generosity is very challenging, and the world does not always reward goodness directly. The noblest people are often scorned. People who are generous, kind and loving are often laughed at. This is the "narrow way," and the "strait gate." It is often easier to do the wrong things and get praise than to do the right things and get criticized. But we must do the right things if we are going to make a good world.

Jesus spoke very frequently against people conducting their lives simply to impress others. In Luke 6:26 he addresses this problem generally.

Woe unto you, when all men shall speak well of you! for so did their fathers to the false prophets.

In Matthew 6:1-4 Jesus discusses the practice of giving alms, or giving charity to those less fortunate than ourselves. Even though being charitable is a good and noble act, Jesus did not want us to give alms publicly, in order to impress others. He wanted us to do so privately, so that the act would be one of pure generosity, not one of expecting praise or even thanks.

Take heed that ye do not your alms before men, to be seen of them: otherwise ye have no reward of your

Father which is in heaven. Therefore when thou doest thine alms, do not sound a trumpet before thee, as the hypocrites do in the synagogues and in the streets, that they may have glory of men. Verily I say unto you, They have their reward. But when thou doest alms, let not thy left hand know what thy right hand doeth: That thine alms may be in secret: and thy Father which seeth in secret himself shall reward thee openly.

When we are giving to charity, it is important to do so from a pure desire to give, not merely to impress people with our generosity. If we give charitably just to impress others we are not giving at all. We are just trying to trade money for positive attention. This is an act that just increases our spiritual poverty.

Many wealthy people today give money to charity purely as a tax write-off. This is not generosity at all. This is greed in sheep's clothing. It may make you feel good for a moment, and make others look upon you favorably, but it in no way builds integrity of character. And ultimately it does not make the world much better.

In Mark 12:43-44 Jesus points out that those who give with a pure heart, even if it is only a small amount, give much more than those give large amounts for the wrong reasons.

Verily I say unto you, That this poor widow hath cast more in, than all they which have cast into the treasury: For all they did cast in of their abundance; but she of her want did cast in all that she had, even all her living.

In Matthew 6:5-8 Jesus discusses the same principle of acting from the right and wrong purpose as it applies to prayer.

> And when thou prayest, thou shalt not be as the hypocrites are: for they love to pray standing in the synagogues and in the corners of the streets, that they may be seen of men. Verily I say unto you, They have their reward. But thou, when thou prayest, enter into thy closet, and when thou hast shut thy door, pray to thy Father which is in secret; and thy Father which seeth in secret shall reward thee openly.

Whenever I read this passage I always think of those evangelical preachers on television who raise their hands in the air and pray for all of us as they are asking us to give them our money out of the other side of their mouths. I'm sure that many of them mean well, but this is not what Jesus wanted at all.

Jesus wanted our relationship with God to be private and sacred, and our relations with our fellow human beings to be inspired by the love and charity that this relationship with God creates. When religious leaders make a great show about their faith and the importance of their work they are doing so to impress other people. God already knows what they have done.

Jesus had something quite instructive to say about misguided religious leaders in Luke 6:39.

> Can the blind lead the blind? shall they not both fall into the ditch?

Humility was of the utmost importance to Jesus, because when we are humble we do not seek to impress others, but instead we seek to serve others. In Matthew 23-11-12 he describes this clearly.

> But he that is greatest among you shall be your servant. And whosoever shall exalt himself shall be abased; and he that shall humble himself shall be exalted.

Jesus was also deeply concerned with our hypocritical adherence to various societal taboos, without being good and pure in our hearts. In Mark 7:15 he addresses this in the form of discussing certain Hebrew regulations regarding washing properly before eating.

> There is nothing from without a man, that entering into him can defile him: but the things which come out of him, those are they that defile the man.

It is not what we put into ourselves that can harm us spiritually; it is what we do inside ourselves that can cause us spiritual harm. It is our inner motivations and our intentions that cause us harm. Jesus describes some of the things we do that can "defile" us in Mark 7:21-23.

> For from within, out of the heart of men, proceed evil thoughts, adulteries, fornications, murders, Thefts, covetousness, wickedness, deceit, lasciviousness, an evil eye, blasphemy, pride, foolishness: All these evil things come from within, and defile the man...

It is not what we do that defines us. It is how we do it and for what reasons. If we follow all of the customs of society, go to church, get married, have a good job, and two and a half children, but inwardly we are filled with hatred, lust, anger, envy and resentment we are no better off than any criminal. This kind of life creates divisions within ourselves and deeply separates us from our brothers and sisters. Even if we appear to be pillars of society, inwardly we are monsters. Many politicians and spiritual leaders have been exposed to be this kind of person, and those exposures deeply damage our collective culture.

On the other hand, if our lives are unusual, our behavior outside of cultural conventions, and we are judged harshly by the majority, but our hearts are filled with love, peace and humility then we are better off than any of these hypocrites. If our relationship with God is pure, our lives are pure. If we are good to other people, we are righteous, even if others judge us wrongly. In Luke 18:10-14 Jesus tells a story that illustrates this point.

Two men went up into the temple to pray; the one a Pharisee, and the other a publican. The Pharisee stood and prayed thus with himself, God, I thank thee, that I am not as other men are, extortioners, unjust, adulterers, or even as this publican. I fast twice in the week, I give tithes of all that I possess. And the publican, standing afar off, would not lift up so much as his eyes unto heaven, but smote upon his breast, saying, God be merciful to me a sinner. I tell you, this man went down to his house justified rather than the other: for every one that exalteth himself shall be abased; and he that humbleth himself shall be exalted.

CHAPTER SIX
THE LIGHT OF THE WORLD

Jesus wanted us to be humble. He did not want us to try to impress others with our piety, our social position, our money, or our prestige, but he wanted our goodness and love to shine forth on the world for all to see. He states this clearly in Matthew 5:14.

Ye are the light of the world.

To make the world a better place we need to become powerful forces of good in the world and treat all people with respect and love. This powerful goodness will be a beacon of light in the universe, and will awaken more people to the light.

We need to reach out to all people with our love, to the poor, to the damaged, to all in need and those in danger of making bad choices. This must be done purely out of a good heart and an honest desire to be helpful. We cannot do so in order to impress others or even in the hopes of persuading anyone that our outlook on life is better or superior to anyone else's. We must simply do it because we are good. We *are* the light of the world. In Matthew 5:16 Jesus elaborates.

Let your light so shine before men, that they may see your good works, and glorify your Father which is in heaven.

Jesus wants us all to be out spreading goodness so that every person will eventually be called to the highest through our light. This light must come from a genuine love for others, and will radiate from you quite automatically when you have devoted yourself to your highest principles. If there is insincerity anywhere within you, you will fool some people and obtain their admiration falsely, but many will recognize your insincerity and you will only confirm their worst fears about humanity. If you wish to have a transformational effect upon the world you must face your own hypocrisy fearlessly, accept it, and in this acceptance you will find yourself becoming transformed. You will discover the true higher principles within you, and you will find your light.

The procedure that Jesus prescribes for discovering and accessing our connection with the light is one of his most mystical instructions. This kind of mystical instruction is fairly rare in the teachings of Jesus, but the following passage is very clearly an instruction in experiencing unity with the divine. In Luke 11:34-36 Jesus describes the method.

> The light of the body is the eye: therefore when thine eye is single, thy whole body also is full of light; but when thine eye is evil, thy body also is full of darkness. Take heed therefore that the light which is in thee be not darkness. If thy whole body therefore be full of light, having no part dark, the whole shall be full of light, as when the bright shining of a candle doth give thee light.

This is the essence of mysticism in a few sentences. When our "eye is single," we are focusing our attention completely on one thing. When the whole focus of our attention is on one single thought, idea, or principle, our whole being transforms. This usually happens in meditation or prayer in which our whole being seems to open up and become filled with the light of the divine. We find our individual consciousness merging with something greater than itself.

But it can also happen anytime in daily life when we become conscious of our higher purpose in life, and take action toward that purpose. Suddenly something opens up within us and we are capable of functioning in new and superior ways. Athletes experience this when they achieve perfection in their sport, artists when they enter the flow of creativity, and even business executives sometimes enter into this state when they see the bigger picture and understand the structures of their business in some new and innovative way. There is often a sense of light that accompanies these experiences even in the world of the mundane.

If we focus our attention on making the world a better place, and devote ourselves single-mindedly to that purpose, new capabilities will grow within us, emerging unexpectedly. We will find ourselves carried by forces greater than ourselves, and our impact on the world will be magnified. The key to this is singleness of purpose and singleness of awareness. Our intentions must also be entirely pure.

The second phrase describes the opposite situation. When our "eye is evil," we are plagued with doubts and worries, or constantly second guessing ourselves, our resources become vastly diminished. Our inner experience becomes dark, as does our expression and countenance.

Our ability to connect with others becomes limited, and our accomplishments are inconsistent.

The same is true if we have hidden agendas. If you wish to help a person in need because you want that person to feel indebted to you, or to join your church or faith, this double purpose will diminish your effectiveness. If on the other hand you simply help the person in need because you are a good and noble being that person will naturally feel drawn to your light and will be transformed more completely by the experience. You will truly make the world a better place. And that person may ask you more about who you are and your beliefs. Then what you say will have real impact.

It is our responsibility to share our love with our fellow beings. When you experience the love-filled light of integrity as a genuine phenomenon a greater feeling of love is a natural occurrence. When you are full of light, that light shines and transforms all that are near. Jesus describes this in the form of a question in Mark 4:21.

> Is a candle brought to be put under a bushel, or under a bed? and not to be set on a candlestick?

There are many people today who are not operating from this singleness of purpose, who have many hidden agendas. These people sometimes come directly in the name of Jesus, but do not share his message of love and forgiveness. Jesus describes these in Matthew 7:15-16

> Beware of false prophets, which come to you in sheep's clothing, but inwardly they are ravening wolves. Ye shall know them by their fruits. Do men gather grapes of thorns, or figs of thistles? Even so

every good tree bringeth forth good fruit; but a corrupt tree bringeth forth evil fruit.

When someone communicates to you about religion, you must ask yourself what it is they are trying to create with their words. What kind of "tree" are they trying to produce? Are they trying to create a more loving world? Or do their teachings encourage hatred? Are they trying to bring people together? Or are they dividing people? Is their message bringing light, or creating more darkness? Jesus expands upon this idea in Luke 6:43-45.

For every tree is known by his own fruit. For of thorns men do not gather figs, nor of a bramble bush gather they grapes. For a good tree bringeth not forth corrupt fruit; neither doth a corrupt tree bring forth good fruit. A good man out of the good treasure of his heart bringeth forth that which is good; and an evil man out of the evil treasure of his heart bringeth forth that which is evil: for of the abundance of the heart his mouth speaketh.

There are many that claim to be spreading the teachings of Jesus in the world but in fact are spreading something other than love and forgiveness. This is a shame as it simply further divides humanity rather than joining us together in universal love and harmony. The message of Jesus was love, a love freely given to all. Jesus wanted us to be the light of the world. Let us try to reach out to one another in true brotherhood, and really make this world a better place.

CHAPTER SEVEN
THE CHILDREN OF GOD

We are all the children of God. Jesus teaches this again and again throughout his ministry. Frequently when Jesus calls us the children of God, he speaks about it as if we will earn this title in the future, when we have accomplished something specific. The essence of what we must accomplish in order to be children of God is exactly what I have been describing throughout this book: a love for each other that we give with all our hearts. We are all the children of God, even if we behave badly, but in order to consider ourselves fully deserving of that title we must behave like children of God. For instance, in Mat 5:9 Jesus explains that wants us to be peacemakers.

Blessed are the peacemakers: for they shall be called the children of God.

Jesus urged us to make peace with each other and with all people. When we see all people as our brothers and sisters, and make peace with them all, we can truly consider ourselves the children of God.

In Matthew 5:44-4 he teaches us the importance of loving our enemies, just as our father in heaven does. Here he directly explains how this will qualify us to consider ourselves the children of God.

Love your enemies, bless them that curse you, do good to them that hate you, and pray for them which despitefully use you, and persecute you; That ye may be the children of your Father which is in heaven: for he maketh his sun to rise on the evil and on the good, and sendeth rain on the just and on the unjust.

God loves all people, so we need to love all people if we want to consider ourselves God's children. He delivers the same message in Luke 6:35, but this time explaining clearly that God is truly loving even to people who are evil.

But love ye your enemies, and do good, and lend, hoping for nothing again; and your reward shall be great, and ye shall be the children of the Highest: for he is kind unto the unthankful and to the evil.

Jesus wanted us all to consider God our father, and to behave as good children of our heavenly father. He wanted us to see God as a good and just, loving father. He says this quite clearly again and again, for instance in Matthew 23:9.

And call no man your father upon the earth: for one is your Father, which is in heaven.

Jesus wanted our actions here on Earth to be a direct reflection of the goodness of our heavenly father. Jesus wanted us to be perfect as God in Matthew 5:48.

Be ye therefore perfect, even as your Father which is in heaven is perfect.

Jesus had the same expectations for his followers that he did for himself. He did not want to be separated from us, but rather for each of us to achieve the love and goodness that he had in himself. Jesus wanted us to be just like him. He makes this quite explicitly clear in Luke 6:40.

The disciple is not above his master: but every one that is perfect shall be as his master.

As I've said before, you don't have to literally believe in a Supreme Being in order to be a good person, or even to be a child of God. We are each the product of our ideals, the sum of our core principles. Our ideals create who we are, and these ideals are of the essence of God. Even if you don't believe in God, if you believe in goodness and love you are still a child of God.

Jesus wanted us all to live in love and peace. And he considered all that live in love and peace to be his own family. He expresses this in Mark 3:35.

For whosoever shall do the will of God, the same is my brother, and my sister, and mother.

And what is the will of God? It is to love each other. Jesus considered it very important not only to consider ourselves the children of God but also to behave with the innocence and humility of children. Jesus considered little children especially sacred, and frequently described them as a model for holiness. In Matthew 19:14 he says that he wants little children to approach him freely because they are a perfect example of holy and loving beings.

Suffer little children, and forbid them not, to come unto me: for of such is the kingdom of heaven.

To Jesus, children were of the same nature as the kingdom of heaven. In Mark 10:15 Jesus states that we need to become like these little children if we are to enter the kingdom of heaven.

Whosoever shall not receive the kingdom of God as a little child, he shall not enter therein.

Jesus considered children to be innocent, humble, giving, honest and simple. This is what he wanted for each of us. Although some people today view children as "little brats," and would find it hard to want to emulate them, this is not the aspect of little children to which Jesus is referring. In particular Jesus emphasizes the humility of children in Matthew 18:4.

Whosoever therefore shall humble himself as this little child, the same is greatest in the kingdom of heaven.

It is this humility that Jesus sees as being of central importance. Openness, honesty, and a desire to learn and serve, these are all qualities of children that Jesus wanted us to emulate. In Mark 10:43-44 Jesus explains the concept of humility as being important to the lack of power structure amongst his followers.

...whosoever will be great among you, shall be your minister: And whosoever of you will be the chiefest, shall be servant of all.

Jesus had a vision of service and humility for all people, a loving service exemplified in the nature of children, so that we may all be the children of God that we truly are.

Chapter Eight
Ask and It Shall be Given

In Luke 11:9-10 Jesus promises his disciples that they will receive everything that they want merely by asking.

> Ask, and it shall be given you; seek, and ye shall find; knock, and it shall be opened unto you. For every one that asketh receiveth; and he that seeketh findeth; and to him that knocketh it shall be opened.

Many preachers use this passage to emphasize the power of prayer, and even encourage their congregations to pray for wealth, prestige, new cars and many other earthly, mundane items. But I hope that you can see by now that this is not the sort of things that Jesus had in mind. In fact, in Luke 11:13 Jesus gets more specific about what it is that he is expecting you to ask for. Jesus does not want you to ask for earthly treasures, he wants you to ask for spiritual treasures, the Holy Spirit.

> If ye then, being evil, know how to give good gifts unto your children: how much more shall your heavenly Father give the Holy Spirit to them that ask him?

Jesus wanted you to ask for the spiritual grace of the Holy Spirit, to seek God, and to knock upon the door to the kingdom of heaven. This is clearly what he meant by the above phrase. He was expecting that we would be asking for spiritual light and wisdom, not new cars. To think otherwise is to utterly contradict the rest of his teachings.

Jesus also emphasizes the power of belief and faith to accomplish miracles in several places. In Mark 9:23 he tells a man that if he will believe then his son can be healed.

If thou canst believe, all things are possible to him that believeth.

In Matthew 17:20 he states another of his most famous doctrines.

If ye have faith as a grain of mustard seed, ye shall say unto this mountain, Remove hence to yonder place; and it shall remove; and nothing shall be impossible unto you.

With just a little faith, a mountain can be moved. He repeats this theme throughout the gospels. Sometimes it is a tree instead of a mountain, but the message is essentially the same. With even the smallest amount of faith, even the most extraordinary things are possible. If you believe that your love can change the world, then it will be so. I believe that love, forgiveness and generosity of spirit can save our country. And we can be examples to the whole world. We must embrace our fellow human beings and help everyone selflessly just as Jesus did. With faith we can heal our nation's wounds.

In Mark 11:24 Jesus discusses the power of belief and prayer.

What things soever ye desire, when ye pray, believe that ye receive them, and ye shall have them.

This passage has been used in numerous New Age success and wealth books to proclaim that even Jesus used the power of "the secret," or "the law of attraction."

But it must be kept in mind that all of these proclamations were made in reference to miraculous healings. In the context of the gospels Jesus is trying to teach his disciples to be healers, and is stating that his disciples must have faith and belief in order to effectively heal. Jesus was by no means proposing that faith and belief be used to accumulate earthly wealth of any kind. Jesus was not telling us to believe in money and worldly success, he was telling us to believe in the power to heal all things that afflict us through the miracle of love. He wanted us to believe in love.

Jesus provides an example of the kind of private prayer that he had in mind for his disciples in Luke 11:2-4. I hope that you will notice the obvious lack of requests for wealth or prosperity. The only material request at all is enough bread to survive another day.

Our Father which art in heaven, Hallowed be thy name. Thy kingdom come. Thy will be done, as in heaven, so in earth. Give us day by day our daily bread. And forgive us our sins; for we also forgive every one that is indebted to us. And lead us not into temptation; but deliver us from evil.

Jesus wanted his followers to be loving healers, seekers after goodness, and children of God who give freely of themselves to all people. He wanted us all to find our real treasures in a life of integrity, a life filled with love and spirit. Those who seek to transform his message of faith and belief into a technique for satisfying greed are missing the point entirely. Let us use the power of faith, belief and prayer to make this world a more loving place. We can truly heal the world by letting love dwell more fully in each of us, and by giving that love freely to everyone we meet. Each and every day ask for more wisdom and light, seek after truth and beauty, and knock on the gate to the kingdom of heaven. All that you could ever really want or need is waiting within.

CHAPTER NINE
A HOUSE DIVIDED

In Matthew 12:25 Jesus makes a very important political statement.

Every kingdom divided against itself is brought to desolation; and every city or house divided against itself shall not stand:

Although Jesus is not talking about America specifically in this statement, his words hold true to this day. We are a deeply divided society. We are divided along political lines, religious lines, social lines, economic lines, racial lines, gender lines, the list could go on and on. And these divisions are destroying us.

The same is true among the many nations of the Earth.

And yet in truth there is more that connects each of us than divides us. We all want the same things. We all want our children to be successful, happy, and to have a better life than we have if possible. We all want to live in comfort and peace. We all want to experience love. We all want to believe that things can get better. We are all trying to do the best that we can in whatever circumstances we find ourselves.

And yet we allow ourselves to be divided into factions and camps, based mostly on things that just don't matter in any real sense. We must stop listening to voices that seek to isolate and alienate. We must start listening to voices that bring us together. These positive and negative voices come both from within ourselves and from without, from the people that we engage with on a day to day basis.

When you hear someone tell you something divisive, something hurtful, something hateful, take a moment to consider whether you really want to accept or be a part of such negativity. When you read negative things in the newspaper or on the internet about people or groups, take some time to consider whether such things are leading us toward a better world, or simply creating unnecessary strife and problems. Try to imagine the world from the other perspective, from your neighbor's perspective, and try to love even those who seem to be your enemies unconditionally. Go out and meet them. Make everyone your friend.

Many people were disturbed by the fact that Jesus frequently sat and ate with sinners. In Luke 5:31 Jesus explains why he chose to spend his time amongst the sinners.

They that are whole need not a physician; but they that are sick.

Jesus chose to spend his time amongst people who were in need, people who made poor life choices, and people who were living unhealthy lives. He didn't do this because he wanted to judge them, he did it because he wanted to love them, and to show them that somebody cared about them. From the context of the story it is clear that he was not preaching at them, but instead just simply spending time with them. Just his loving presence gave them healing.

Instead of feeling hostile toward people who live a different kind of life than you do, why not try following the example of Jesus and spend some time with different people. You may find that you actually have more common ground than you think. And you may find that your presence is healing, that your love may call a "sinner to repentance."

On the other hand, when you meet with people from different backgrounds, you may discover that they have some special love in their hearts for you, and that their presence in your life may be a healing opportunity for you.

When you experience someone giving you a message of love and peace, please consider this message even if it is coming from someone you normally would see quite differently. Even if such a message comes from someone you might usually consider your enemy, or someone whose values are different, or whose political ideology is not the same as yours, perhaps this person could actually be a great friend. Jesus taught us to love everybody. He said this again and again throughout his ministry. Love God, Love your neighbors and love your enemies.

It is possible for people who have different views to still be your beloved brothers and sisters. It is possible to forgive anything that you choose to forgive. And Jesus promised that you will receive a great treasure when you do so. The treasure that you will receive is a heart more open to love, and a key to the kingdom of heaven.

When you are feeling angry or resentful in your own heart, when the messages of division are coming from within, take a few moments and consider where such thoughts are leading you. Are they leading toward the kingdom of heaven? Are they leading you toward your own goals? Are those negative thoughts and feelings going to make the world a better place?

When you feel the urge to be kind to someone or to help someone in some way, do so. Even if your kindness is unacknowledged you are still adding to the sum total of goodness in the world.

We are going to have to start working together if we are going to fix the problems of the world. This will mean Christians working hand in hand with atheists and all other religions. This will mean conservatives working hand in hand with liberals. This will mean all people of every nationality, background and belief system finding common ground. This will mean putting aside differences in order to work toward our shared goals. And I believe that the best place to start is simply with love. We all love our world, our country, and our children. So let's start from this place of love that we all share.

I don't necessarily know you personally, but I want to be your friend. I hope you'll be my friend. I hope that together, hand in hand, we can make this world a better place. I believe that we can create the beautiful kingdom that Jesus envisioned. I don't expect you to agree with me all the time, and I don't expect you to love me as much as I love you. That wouldn't be fair. Just as Jesus did, I only want to express to the whole world that I love you with all my heart.

All we need to save our country is for you to open your heart as much as you are able. I want you to know that I care about you, and I care about the future of this world. Together we can enter the kingdom as soon as you are ready.

CHAPTER TEN
THE CROWD CHOSE BARABBAS

I want to touch upon one final subject before concluding. This topic is not about the teachings of Jesus directly, but rather about how his teachings were received by the crowds during his life. At first, Jesus and his teachings were received quite favorably by many, and large crowds assembled to hear him speak. Many thought that Jesus might be the messiah they were waiting for, the powerful holy king who would rid Israel of the Romans that had occupied the Holy Land. But the story told in Matthew, Mark and Luke contains a final incident in the life of Jesus that has always struck me deeply, and frequently makes me cry when I think about it.

When Jesus came to Jerusalem for the final time, the people were expecting him to overthrow their oppressors, to conquer the Romans and the false king Herod, perhaps with an army of angels. But instead he simply nonviolently allowed himself to be arrested. He was accused of treason, of proclaiming himself king, of proclaiming himself the son of God. He did not even try to defend himself in court. Pontius Pilate did not know what to do with him.

Meanwhile, another man was arrested, a man named Barabbas. Barabbas was involved in a violent attempt to overthrow the government. He was a revolutionary, a rebel, some modern translations of the Bible call him a terrorist. He was accused of both treason and murder.

Pontius Pilate asked the crowd gathered in Jerusalem which savior they would rather release, the violent murderer, or the peaceful preacher. In the end, the crowd chose Barabbas.

The crowd chose Barabbas because they thought that he, unlike Jesus, would actually free them from their bondage to Rome. The crowd chose what they believed was the easy path. They felt that violence was the best path to freedom, and that Barabbas was a man of action, while Jesus was a weak pacifist. The powerful elite of Jerusalem encouraged the crowd in this, because Jesus was a great threat to the status quo. The message of love and unity that Jesus preached was dangerous to the rich and powerful, whose power was based on fear and division. They wanted to be rid of Jesus. And the rich and powerful got their way. After all, Barabbas never freed the Jews, and the elite kept all their power.

Nothing has changed in two thousand years. The rich and powerful still control the crowds with fear and division, and the loving message of Jesus is still a great threat to the status quo.

We are all that crowd, and we all get to make that choice between Jesus and Barabbas in our hearts again and again. When we choose violence, fear and anger we are choosing Barabbas all over again. When we choose love, unity and forgiveness, we are instead choosing Jesus.

When we vote in elections, if we vote for candidates who want to solve our struggles with war and destruction, we are choosing Barabbas. If we choose candidates who seek peaceful solutions, who want to create peace and love in the world, we are choosing Jesus.

When we are violent with our children, our families, our friends, we are choosing Barabbas, and teaching our loved ones to choose Barabbas too. When we are thoughtful, generous, loving, gracious and forgiving, we teach everyone to choose Jesus.

The choices that we make today will affect the whole course of history. Now is the time for good people to wake up, stand up, and start taking action to make this world a better place. We all need to become leaders. We can save our country. We can do this through the power of love that Jesus taught, or we can try to save our country through violence, aggression and force. Choose well brothers and sisters, because our future depends on it.

About the Author

Jason Newcomb has been fascinated with the religions of the world since childhood. He has deeply studied many religions and philosophies from around the world. Every religion has many differences with other religions, but there is one thread that they all have in common. All religions consider one thing to be of the greatest importance: the power of love.

Jason has devoted his life to helping others to transform their lives, to discover that each of us has limitless possibilities, and to recognize that most of the roadblocks that we experience in life are the ones we create ourselves. He knows that every human being has nearly limitless possibilities and that by unlocking the latent power in our own minds we can access transformations in every part of our lives. He is devoted to helping individuals and groups to become the absolute most that they can be. He wants to see everyone live life as fully and joyfully as they truly can imagine.

Jason Newcomb is a licensed practitioner of Neuro-Linguistic Programming through the Society of NLP, a certified hypnotherapist through the American Board of Hypnotherapy, and a member of the advisory board of the American Alliance of Hypnotists.

He is also a writer, artist and occasional filmmaker who lives in Southwest Florida with his amazing wife Jennifer and his beautiful daughter Aurora.

www.newcombcoaching.com

ABOUT

LIGHT A CANDLE
BOOKS

Light a Candle Books publishes motivational, inspirational and educational books for a diverse contemporary audience. We hope that you have enjoyed this book and will look forward to future releases.

www.ingramcontent.com/pod-product-compliance
Lightning Source LLC
LaVergne TN
LVHW091205080426
835509LV00006B/833